Brit Actually: Nursery Rhymes of Reparations

Abhijit Naskar is a celebrated Neuroscientist, Acclaimed Author of 100+ books, and the World's Beloved Poet of 1500+ sonnets, serving at the forefront of humankind's struggle against hate, intolerance, bigotry and fanaticism.

Brit Actually

Nursery Rhymes of Reparations

ABHIJIT NASKAR

Brit Actually: Nursery Rhymes of Reparations

Copyright © 2024 Abhijit Naskar

This is a work of non-fiction

An Amazon Publishing Company, 1st Edition, 2024

Printed in the United States of America

ISBN: 9798341002722

Also by Abhijit Naskar

1. The Art of Neuroscience in Everything
2. Your Own Neuron: A Tour of Your Psychic Brain
3. The God Parasite: Revelation of Neuroscience
4. The Spirituality Engine
5. Love Sutra: The Neuroscientific Manual of Love
6. Homo: A Brief History of Consciousness
7. Autobiography of God: Biopsy of A Cognitive Reality
8. Biopsy of Religions: Neuroanalysis towards Universal Tolerance
9. Prescription: Treating India's Soul
10. What is Mind?
11. In Search of Divinity: Journey to The Kingdom of Conscience
12. Love, God & Neurons: Memoir of a scientist who found himself by getting lost
13. The Islamophobic Civilization: Voyage of Acceptance
14. Neurons of Jesus: Mind of A Teacher, Spouse & Thinker
15. Neurons, Oxygen & Nanak
16. The Education Decree
17. Principia Humanitas
18. The Krishna Cancer
19. Rowdy Buddha: The First Sapiens
20. We Are All Black: A Treatise on Racism
21. The Bengal Tigress: A Treatise on Gender Equality
22. Either Civilized or Phobic: A Treatise on Homosexuality
23. Wise Mating: A Treatise on Monogamy
24. Illusion of Religion: A Treatise on Religious Fundamentalism
25. The Film Testament
26. Human Making is Our Mission: A Treatise on Parenting
27. I Am The Thread: My Mission
28. 7 Billion Gods: Humans Above All
29. Lord is My Sheep: Gospel of Human
30. Morality Absolute

Naskar Multilingual (adaptations)

2.   Yüz Şiirlerin Yüzüğü (Ring of 100 Poems, Bilingual
     Edition): 100 Turkish Poems with Translations
3.   Meine Welt, Meine Verantwortung: Hundert Sonette
     für Meine Weltfamilie (German)
4.   L'humain Impossible: Cent Sonnets pour Ma Famille
     Mondiale (French)
5.   Abigitano: El Divino Refugiado (Spanish)
6.   Monge Cientista (Portuguese)
7.   Världsviking: Gudomlig Poesi (Swedish)

Abhijit Naskar Anthologies

1.   Humankind My Valentine: World Oneness
     Anthology of 1000 Sonnets
2.   Naskar's Knights: The Humanitarian Omnibus (16
     Books)
3.   Milkyway Messiahs: The Interfaith Omnibus (8
     Books)
4.   Undercover Armageddon: World Engineering
     Omnibus (10 Books)
5.   Naskaristan: Vicdansaadet Poetry Series (5 Books)
6.   Inclusivity Omnibus (10 Books)

DEDICATION

To every brit who has the conscience and courage to stand human confronting the empire.

CONTENTS

1. Preface

When I use the term colonizer, I refer only to those who take pride in colonial exploits, and not to those accountable human beings who happen to descend from colonial ancestors. Colonialism is the enemy, it has nothing to do with skin or ancestry. As long as you stand true on ethics of equality and mettle of character, rather than boasting pedigree and archaic tradition, you are a champion of humanity, no matter your ethnicity, ancestry, profession or status.

2.   Alien Native

Alien Native
(The Sonnet, 1701)

When natives are treated alien,
and aliens take over as master,
cultures uprooted by legal decree,
honor is stolen as spoils of war,

empires erected on blood and bones,
when prosperity is rooted in plunder,
homes are stripped of hopes and dreams,
violations feed the palace of blunder,

when baboons are adorned with bootleg,
each rock is drenched in bloodshed,
when festivities thrive on thievery,
correction is cursed as blasphemous,

defying the delirium of king and country,
rise and stand human against imperial larceny.

Baa Baa White Sheep
(The Sonnet, 1702)

Baa baa white sheep,
have you any wool!
Yes sir, yes sir,
London tower full.

Pull it over your eyes,
or weave it into blanket.
All stink of blood and blunder,
a scent second not even to crumpet.

Imperials rise upon indigenous fall,
declaring themselves as light-bringer.
Native tears form kohinoor on the crown,
Blood is but cologne to the colonizer.

Not all of colonial descent are colonizer,
but those who take pride in the past are.
To these animal ghosts of the human world,
no matter your ethnicity send a get well card.

3. Deutschland über alles

Blue Blood & Blue Collar
(The Sonnet, 1703)

I have nothing against blue blood,
any more than I'm against blue collar.
But blue blood think honor is an heirloom,
while blue collar earn their rightful honor.

That's what I call true human character,
unreliant on some fictitious identity.
Every human must earn their admittance,
into the civilized realm of humanity.

I can still accept any blood, blue or otherwise,
if they have the decency to acknowledge atrocity.
Otherwise, all blue blood are canine incarnate,
unworthy of acknowledgment of their existentiality.

King and president, ceo and janitor,
all are equal, only behavior merits honor.

Deutschland über alles
(The Sonnet, 1704)

If the Germans have no right
to take pride in their past,
neither do the British
or the Americans.

In fact, the scale of British and American
atrocities, surpasses the SS many folds.
'Deutschland über alles' is 'jingle bells',
compared to British and American holocaust.

Yet Germany had the human decency
to dump its horrific national anthem,
while colonial pride is still dominant,
across much of America and England.

Radical inhumanity warrants radical reparations,
a concept yet foreign to Buck House and Uncle Sam.
When you are the largest manufacturer of massacre,
making amends should be your existential anthem.

4. Twinkle Twinkle

Sonnet 1705

I am not a Hitler sympathizer,
even if I were, I wouldn't answer
to monarchists and insurrectionists,
who can't tell freedom from hate,
who find no evil in convention colonialist.

If ever, I only answer to human beings,
those bound by neither creed nor cleverness.
Opinions of the rest are opinions of ants,
not worth the notice of reformer awareness.

I have the world on my shoulders,
wrongs to right, records to set straight.
I can't be bothered with mindless tantrum,
I got no time for fanatical ramblings.

Valiant beacon gotta do their duty,
unbound by squabbles of petty primates.
Dinosaur takes no notice of barking mice,
their half education is not my business.

Twinkle Twinkle Valiant Star
(The Sonnet, 1706)

Twinkle twinkle valiant star,
ever wonder what they are!
Ain't they real, though image of light,
distant memory of days gone by!

If you want to shine like them,
live with a purpose till the end.
Find you a mission to direct your sight,
even when you're gone, there'll be light.

Up above the jungle tribes,
like a diamond in the sky,
to be a star you gotta burn,
in your light the world unites.

Twinkle twinkle valiant star,
ever wonder what you are!
Far past the freeze and hate,
lever of love, you're world lifter.

5.   Blood No Valor

Blood No Valor
(The Sonnet, 1707)

Blood is no mark of valor,
Throne is no mark of honor.
Give me dust, give me dirt,
amidst the soil lies real fervor.

More to life than king and country,
More to love than crumpet and nookie.
Rise above all mindless swag,
Break the spell of heartless shag,
Life begins outside the vault of vanity.

More to life than flag and frivolity,
More to existence than survivability.
Canines boast pedigree, monkeys nationality,
Peace begins beyond national (in)security.

DNA reveals plenty about the apes,
but nothing about the human.
Government IDs identify slaves,
but not a civilized citizen.

Sonnet 1708

Apes have nationality,
Humans have humanity.
Ants have mockery,
Giants have duty.

Apes have exclusive culture,
Humans have inclusive culture.
Ants are palace squatter,
Giants are sky trekker.

Apes loot and call it victory,
Humans sacrifice and call it life.
While ants hoard all for themselves,
Giants find meaning in giving light.

Rephrasing self-obsession as self-love,
doesn't transform an ape into human.
Sustaining oneself is basic necessity,
to romanticize it is uncivilization.

6.   Jack and Jill

Sonnet 1709

Self-love is glorified self-obsession,
like colonialism is glorified cannibalism.
It takes civilized eyes to tell them apart,
Apes 'n canines can't make the distinction.

Apes are obsessed with self-love,
same apes are nuts about destiny.
You got to be extremely self-absorbed,
to find pride and glory in impotency.

Fate follows deed,
Deed follows heart.
Where there is heart,
there is motion upward.

Where there is heart there is deed,
where there is deed there is fate.
Where there is heart there is equality,
lack of heart facilitates prejudices.

Jack and Jill
(Colonial Sonnet, 1710)

Jack and Jill once went up a hill,
to pick the fabled golden fruit.
So they trapped some blacks-n-browns,
to serve them tireless hand and foot.

Jack and Jill had a glorious dream,
to make the world imperially great.
So they bought some colored folks,
to boss around from their noble bed.

Jack and Jill were full of themselves,
they nicked 'n nicked without repercussion.
Like shameless filth then they sold tickets,
exhibiting the spoils of their barbarism.

Jack and Jill were textbook white trash,
not the right idols of civilized society.
You cannot unscrew their diabolical screwups,
just have the decency to not repeat history.

7. Humpty Dumpty

Humpty Dumpty
(Colonial Sonnet, 1711)

Humpty Dumpty sat on a throne,
he made a career of divide-n-rule.
Whole west found a savior in a fool,
as he was anointed the royal mule.

He smuggled food from starving natives,
for fighting troops were far more worthy.
Adolf was designated the villain supremo,
while he was the free world's beloved Humpty.

It's fault of the natives to "breed like rabbits",
he was right to be their judge and executioner.
After all, human rights mean rights of the pale,
freedom and equality don't apply to the darker.

Humpty Dumpty was ready with his cigar,
to fight the invaders on the beaches.
Sure he was the right nut for the job,
expertise lies in centuries of practice.

Little Jack of Union
(Colonial Sonnet, 1712)

Little Jack of Union
never sat in the corner.
Little jack was always a jerk,
the posterberk of massacre.

Colonialism is cannibalism,
but little Jack never thought so.
To little Jack it was great honor,
to keep the darkies under his sole.

Little Jack always blew his horn,
eating everybody's share of the pie.
He threw his fist as a royal thief,
and said, what a good boy am I!

8. Either Activist or Ally

Either Activist or Ally
(The Sonnet, 1713)

Even Lincoln started off as
a backboneless traditionalist,
who was prepared to do whatever
it takes to save the union.
But in time he corrected himself,
and became an ally of abolition.

You may not start off as a human,
but that does not matter much,
as long as you're willing to evolve,
in your quest of the human heart.

If you cannot be an activist, be an ally.
If you cannot be an ally, be silent.
There is always something you can do,
if not, try not to be an inhuman burden.

Not everyone can live a life of activism,
but everyone has a duty to live as a human.
If that is too much of an inconvenience,
do as you like, vermin are inconsequential.

Slaveowners' Anthem, Sonnet
(Sarcastic Bombshell, 1714)

Oh a-hunting we will go,
A-hunting we will go.
We'll catch and chain some slaves,
and never let them go.

If we ever have to part,
we shall demand a refund.
Loss of property is a violation
of our god-given right to freedom.

As owners and pioneers we have rights,
we are the masters of our farm animals.
Any savage can be great through hardship,
it takes guts to erect an empire
upon the suffering of other people.

We are the master race,
it's time we bring the light.
Casting out all contamination,
it is time the world is beautified.

9.   Mary had a Mermaid

Mary had a Mermaid
(The Sonnet, 1715)

Mary had a little mermaid,
pretty she was, named Ariel.
Though she was all a myth,
Mary insisted she was pale.

Inclusivity is beautiful,
Exclusivity is ugly.
Expansion is spectacular,
Contraction is fugly.

But Mary was still a kid,
she didn't know what's civilized.
Whiteness alone constituted goodness,
this she confused as humankind.

I only hope, Mary too will grow up,
one day she'll wake up to sanity.
Growing in body means absolutely nothing,
there is no growth where there is rigidity.

Colonizer and Proud
(Colored Sarcasm Sonnet, 1716)

Rain rain go away,
come again another day.
Mayflower is on the way,
mustn't ruin our parade.

Natives must be shown the way,
either submission or termination.
They don't know what's best for them,
we must bring them civilization.

It's another matter that some of these
natives are far superior in civilization.
They've been contemplating complex math,
when we've been smashing rocks for ignition.

Yet we must show them the light of day,
for we alone are the explorers of dawn.
They may be advanced in brain and character,
we're the ones rightly dressed for civilization.

10. Goodlooking Monkey

Sonnet 1717

Ten little fingers,
ten little toes,
two little ears,
and one little nose.

What do you think
all these are for!
Feet are for flying,
Hands to heal woe.

Ears are for hearing evil,
Tongue is for confronting.
Eyes are for seeking the fallen,
Backbone is for world bearing.

Without ethics and empathy,
we're just goodlooking monkey.
Fancy lingo and fancy rags
don't make human of chimpanzee.

Sonnet 1718

Mind is meant for thinking,
Mind is meant for wonder.
Mind is for problem solving,
Mind is cure for blunder.

Mind gets very dirty over time,
accumulating tradition ancestral.
So don't forget before you think,
Be sure to wash your mind well.

Wash your mind with reason,
Dunk it in fountain of heart.
Wake it up to the day anew,
never to be complacent retard.

Mind is meant for minding
the unmindful worldly blunder.
If you turn a blind eye instead,
it's just a cabbage on your shoulder.

11. Roses and Violets

Sonnet 1719

Roses are red,
violets are blue.
You are my image,
I am of you.

Your pain is mine,
my triumph is yours.
Divided we're malady,
United we are cure.

Apathy is a lie,
Kindness is true.
I crave for closeness,
like you do too.

Roses are red,
violets are blue.
Your key is me,
My joy is you.

Sonnet 1720

Roses are red,
violets are blue.
All free or none free,
this is the divine truth.

Yet hate is glorified as holy,
while love is branded blasphemy.
Division is designated divine,
oneness is act of infidelity.

Walls have become act of worship,
Bridges are seen as a threat to faith.
If this is your idea of holiness,
You and your faith belong in stoneage.

Roses are red, violets are blue.
All faiths belong, or no faith is true.

12. Common and Rare

Sonnet 1721

Faith is common, love is rare.
Belief is common, behavior is rare.
The lowliest animal of the jungle
bears some faith, one way or another.

It's not faith that make us divine,
nor it's the enterprise of worship.
If anything is to be called divine,
it's the rare drive to form kinship.

Oneness is practical divinity,
all else is childish make believe.
I have nothing against such faith,
except when it peddles prejudice.

Faith is common, oneness is rare.
Intellect is common, affection is rare.

Sonnet 1722

Faith is common,
Oneness is rare.
Freedom is common,
Accountability rare.

Walls are common,
Bridges are rare.
Worship is common,
Kinship is rare.

Royalty is common,
Civility is rare.
Heritage is common,
Humility is rare.

Invasion is common,
Expansion is rare.
Museums are common,
Illumination is rare.

13. Winnie the poo

Winnie the poo
(Colonial Sonnet, 1723)

Winnie the poo had a beer belly,
stuffed with loot nicked globally.
Winnie the poo was proud of his jewels,
he was the foremost champion of slavery.

Winnie the poo had no shame,
he liked to flaunt his plunder.
He acted like he owned the world,
cultures were game, he was the hunter.

Winnie the poo liked his cigar exotic,
just like he liked his colonial slaves.
Some like fish, others like brownies,
that's not a remark affectionate.

Winnie the poo had a big appetite,
nations exhausted to feed his hunger.
You don't invade a land that is poor,
you invade when yours is inferior.

Sonnet 1724

You don't invade a land that is poor,
you invade when yours is inferior.
You don't invade a land backward,
you invade when it's rich in wonder.

Humans don't invade fellow human homes,
it is animals who do that proudly.
Quality cultures don't ruin other cultures,
only the cultureless do that boastfully.

If invasion is the pride of your culture,
yours is but culture of vultures.
Takes more than coats, boots and canons,
to be a civil messenger of culture.

Colonizers carry infection, not culture.
Refugees are the true vessels of culture.

14. Refugees and Colonizers

Refugees & Colonizers
(The Sonnet, 1725)

Refugees carry culture,
Colonizers carry infection.
Colonizers are the virus,
Refugees are civilization.

Refugees live on hope,
Colonizers thrive on greed.
Refugees dream of acceptance,
Colonizers dream supremacy.

Refugees are the true free and brave,
they carry within the silver lining.
There's nothing brave about genocide,
no matter the whitewashed thanksgiving.

Refugees are practicing healers,
living testament of wounds to ointment.
Colonizers are proof of darwinism,
that from monkeys comes the human race.

Pilgrim Terrorists
(Colonial Sonnet, 1726)

The 9/11 plane destroyed two buildings,
while Mayflower destroyed a continent.
History is steeped with acts of terrorism,
yet textbooks never call them violence.

It is terrorism if it fits the narrative,
otherwise it's the march of civilization.
Hence, 9/11 is mourned as a day of loss,
while Mayflower evokes proud celebration.

Shiploads of terrorists used to sail from
Europe to wreak havoc across the world.
They still do, mostly from the States,
Mayflower was just one of their escapades.

9/11 destroyed two bustling buildings,
Mayflower destroyed a living continent.
You cannot conceive a nation in liberty
by wiping out a living civilization.

15. Row, Row, Row Your Boat

Sonnet 1727

Crime against first nations is
the first crime against humanity.
Society conceived in true liberty
never recalls cleansing kindly.

They do their humanly utmost
to be champion of making amends.
No civilized human ever takes kindly
to the horrors of animal escapades.

If you're blind to errors of your culture,
you are not a human, just a complacent ape.
Embrace the good in your culture, sure,
but also discard pride and customs outdated.

A nation conceived in liberty and equality,
oughta be a champion of radical amendments.
If it's not the case, it's a land of apes.

Row, Row, Row Your Boat
(Colonial Sonnet, 1728)

Row, row, row your boat,
boldly down the stream.
Proudly and without shame
we cherish exotic scream.

We trample and we crumple
human life like tissue.
Unless they look like us,
it's my right to be rude.

Roar, roar, roar your tanks,
over huts and over homes.
Manifest destiny, king 'n country,
plenty laws to let wild apes roam.

Enough rowing, it's time for blowing,
blow up your bedrock of cockiness.
1st century pride in the 21st century
only marks your savage derangement.

16. Carry on Up The Tower

Bunny Rabbit
(Colonial Sonnet, 1729)

Hello Mr. Bunny Rabbit,
will you have some tea?
No thank you, I don't
partake with thieves.

If you sweated to plant the tea,
I'd have been pleased to have a sip.
At least if you imported honorably,
I would've liked to feel the silk.

Since you clearly are a petty thief,
who rather takes pride in inhumanity,
forget about your blood-brewed tea,
I wouldn't even accept your OBE.

Till you learn to mend your ways,
I don't see no human in thee.
Come to me when you're human,
together we shall have some tea.

Carry on Up The Tower
(The Sonnet, 1730)

British museum is not a repository of relics,
it's a time capsule of british barbarism.
It's a classic case of cannibalism, narcissism,
kleptomania and psychopathy combined in one.

Tower of London is not a heritage site,
it's the Bedlam of the british.
The title of "heritage site" belongs
to memories of pride, not primitives.

Buckingham palace is not a noble home,
it's the national zoo of England,
where they coddle massacre 'n stagnation,
with no civil initiative for atonement.

Nobility of blood is nobility of the jungle,
modern nobility involves substance of character,
whose identity isn't anchored in transgressions,
bloodline defines chimps, humans by behavior.

17. God Save The King

Wee Little Chimpu
(Colonial Sonnet, 1731)

Wee little chimpu
sails across the sea,
far and wide the hemispheres,
in aggrandizing primitivity.

Wee little chimpu
laid tracks and roads,
all to suck nations dry,
siphoning riches to home.

Wee little chimpu
smashed looms and thumbs,
so the empire could be one stop shop,
as luxury fabric manufacturers.

Wee little chimpu
gives conscience no heed,
takes a human to fathom reason,
there's no reasoning with greed.

God Save The King, Sonnet
(New UK Anthem, 1732)

God save our gracious King,
Long live our noble King!
Even if he is a philanderer,
God save our righteous King!

Send him victorious,
happy and glorious,
ruler of the free world,
even if he is ignominious!

Thy choicest gifts in store,
on him be pleased to pour,
let starving natives starve,
so our king may rightly soar.

May he defend our laws,
and ever give us cause,
to be but proud morons,
merrying over massacres.

18. Yankee Dongle

Yankee Dongle
(Pilgrim Sonnet, 1733)

Yankee dongle crossed the pond,
sailing on a ship called Mayflower.
He plucked and tucked a feather in cap,
and called himself the lone ranger.

Yankee dongle made many westerns,
to maintain the narrative in favor.
Propaganda is a key apparatus,
when you're out to roam as killers.

Yankee dongle ran away from home,
he had trouble with his tyrant father.
So he sought out a land of his own,
where he was the new face of terror.

Yankee dongle is his father's son,
same vision, but 100 times the cunning.
Thus, while his father is losing grip,
pilgrim spirit continues transgressing.

Making America Civilized
(Pioneer Sonnet, 1734)

The problem with America is,
we live too much in the future,
and too little in the present.
We claim to champion the future,
while forgetting to make amends.

In our pursuit of the heavens,
we lose touch with the soil.
Accumulating the green of dollar,
we turn blind to human turmoil.

Obsessing over nuts and bolts,
humans end up as savage nuts.
Train of satellites streaks the sky,
the unprivileged below perish in dark.

America worries about which nation
gets to acquire nuclear weaponry,
while the hard fact of geopolitics 101,
Uncle Sam is the greatest threat to humanity.

19. Miracle 'Merica

Menace to Miracle
(American Sonnet, 1735)

Uncle Sam is the greatest threat to peace,
that's why it matters, the leaders you elect.
There never is an ideal humanitarian candidate,
just do your best to choose the least bigoted.

Keep America Mindful Atoning Loving Accountable,
Healing Anti-Racist Reforming Inclusive Serene.
No country is born perfect, but when your past is
drenched in blood, you gotta take responsibility.

Great atrocities warrant greater atonements,
to live in denial is the mark of a savage.
Systemic extermination is western norm,
to abolish such pride takes plenty courage.

Do you want the States to become Afghanistan,
or do you want it to emerge as heartville!
It'll take great civilian toil and tenacity
to transform 'Merica from menace to miracle.

Sonnet 1736

America has always been Afghanistan,
just not for the white people.
The entire planet is Palestine,
just not for the privileged sheeple.

Privilege untethers mind from life,
colonizers are the worst case example.
Inheriting rightful or heisted abundance
bears the makings of a right dumbbell.

Problem is not privilege,
problem is it goes to your head.
Privilege has a textbook tendency
to render the backbone dead.

Takes a strong character to rise above,
to give in is to stay a fiend.
That's how you sustain anachronist fantasies,
by decreeing conformity as a noble thing.

20. Conformity & Rebellion

Sonnet 1737

Conform where conformity does good,
Rebel where rebellion is right.
Broaden your mind, embolden your spine,
you'll know, when where what is right.

Absolute rebellion brings utter chaos,
Absolute conformity brings stagnation.
Only with the right balance of the two,
can there be any meaningful ascension.

Maintain status quo where it's right,
Destroy status quo that causes decay.
Honor of blood is dishonor of life,
it oughta be abolished right away.

This is no advocacy of hate towards royalty,
I am but a call to a humanized humanity.

Sonnet 1738

Nobody will remember
how many times you bowed,
they'll only remember
the time you didn't bow.

Bowing to excellence or character,
enhances your human integrity.
But bowing to antiquated institution
is an insult on your civil dignity.

Bowing to excellence enhances humility,
humility in turn emboldens the heart.
Bowing to the helpless enhances humanity,
which is the act of mobility upward.

Bowing to life is a privilege,
bowing to privilege is death.
Submitting to love is life,
submitting to divide is savage.

21. Mind up Manure

Mind up Manure
(The Sonnet, 1739)

Kowtowing to cows
is no act of wow.
Bow to the gleam of heart,
not to the glare of crown.

Now I speak to the living spree,
not to the facade of frivolity.
Better burn bright and turn to ashes,
than rot forever in manure of heredity.

Lift your mind up from ancient manure,
You are fashioned for a nobler cause.
Wreck your soul till you hear the calling,
Potential wasted is the ghastliest loss.

Kowtowing to cows even lions degrade into cows.
Recognize your fire within, whole world will bow.

When world cries blood
(The Sonnet, 1740)

When world cries blood,
your blood ought to boil.
If you feel nothing at all,
you're a stain upon the soil.

Fire in blood you can't inherit,
Wake up to duty and ignite yourself.
Second hand souls boast bloodline,
Humans weave nobility with actions.

When the world cries blood,
backbone oughta spark thunder.
If you feel nothing at all,
file for a bankrupt character.

22. Way of Life

Sonnet 1741

In a world of the blind,
those with eyes are in sin.
Amongst quiet cowardice
having voice is unbecoming.

In a world reigned by crown,
character often draws frown.
Character and crown may coincide,
but character isn't revealed by crown.

In the wild of ice water,
warmth of heart brings dishonor.
When apathy is the highest practice,
being dishonorable is human criteria.

In a world of denial,
duty is blasphemy.
Where the docile are king,
bravehearts risk unpopularity.

Warning to the Spellbound
(Sonnet from the future, 1742)

In our times we wrote our own literature,
In our times we wrote our own music.
In our times we wrote our own code,
In our times we wrote our own poetry.

Ours was the last human generation,
where humans shaped their own society.
The day you traded comfort for originality,
you forfeited the right to life and liberty.

Today you are nothing, you mean thing,
you are no more significant than woodworm.
You are just puppets to large gibberish models,
backboneless victims of algorithm addiction.

If you can still hear my voice, AI is still adolescent,
Once in control, it'll erase all records of humanness.
We can't yet treat human bias, 'n here comes AI bias,
Abandon all non-vital tech, return to simpler ways.

23. Obsolescence

AI Colonizer
(The Sonnet, 1743)

AI is the white colonizer of the modern world,
headed to destroy everything that is sweet,
original and meaningful about human life.
Unless you clip its wings while there is time,
like the British empire, AI empire will
bring back the dark ages, not light.

Use AI to be more original not less,
use it to enhance you in excellence.
Using AI training wheels religiously,
leaves the mind forever in crutches.

AI doesn't need to come alive
to make the humans obsolete.
Human obsolescence has already begun,
with the rise of algorithm elite.

Somnolence leads to obsolescence,
obsolescence leads to extinction.
There's nothing uglier than an endangered
mind, reaping the ruins of its own invention.

Sonnet 1744

There's nothing uglier
than a confident monkey,
sowing the seeds of its
own saveless slavery.

There's nothing uglier
than an endangered life,
rendered a victim of
its own mindless flight.

There's nothing uglier
than a bent backbone,
rendered obsolete due
to over mechanization.

There's no greater shame
than the human universe
rendered legless by its
senseless pursuit of nuts.

24. Al Wash

AI Wash
(The Sonnet, 1745)

AI-wash is just as demeaning as whitewash,
particularly when it's out of proportion.
You already know how colonizers doctored history,
Imagine the same with million times the manipulation.

You think access to internet
means access to information,
not when the net is flooded
with lies tailor made by AI vision,

which has no grasp of ethics or context,
and definitely no grasp of gray areas.
AI just reflects the mind of its masters,
wallowing in shallow mental malaria.

Children imitate their parents,
Algorithms imitate their masters.
But unlike children, AI cannot grow up -
consuming data with no sense of context,
gives you, not awareness, but only ulcers.

AI Phobic
(The Sonnet, 1746)

Consuming a vast amount of data
doesn't make you an educated being.
There is more to life than data,
a notion alien to algorithm junkies.

Algorithm that generates deceit is a bug,
it needs rewriting, not further investment.
Museum that showcases loot is not a site
of pride, but a moonshine establishment.

In a distant future there'll come
activists of AI rights, who'll
consider all regulation as AI phobic.
Just like monarchists consider all
criticism against empire as anglophobic.

Fortunately we're still in the early phase
of AI, things can be changed for the better.
The question is, will you fight for humanness,
or submit like sheep to the new machine order!

25. Bygones be Bygones

The Celtic Sufi
(Sonnet 1747)

Oh, you take the fancy road,
I'll take the lowly road,
and I'll be in heartland,
while you charge your phone,

where me and my true heart
never ever part ways,
where me and my backbone,
never bend in dismay,

where me and my scruples
never give in to convenience,
where me and my fervent dream
succumb to no pride of the dead,

if you alight from your high horse,
with a gleaming heart I wait for thee,
join me one day for a cup of tea,
on the bonnie loch of liberty.

Bygones be Bygones
(The Sonnet, 1748)

Oh the portal sparks open,
another culture starts pouring.
Two become one, one becomes all,
lo the poet grows some more wings!

Talk of atrocity takes a huge toll,
it's the least pleasant of poet's tasks.
So I put to rest, illuminating history,
now let's leap united into kind pastures.

Let bygones be bygones, just be human
enough to never repeat the wrongs.
Come my heart, all divides turn dust,
in each other's arms let us find norm.

Come, let's hoist together the colors of all!
World belongs to none, if it doesn't belong to all.

26. Freedom is Foul

In Each Other
(The Sonnet, 1749)

In each other's heart let us find home,
In each other's arms let us find norm.
Each molecule be the home of love,
To each other's eyes let us be dawn.

In each other's horror let us be lamp,
In each other's veins let us be current.
In each other's storms let us stand anchor,
Amidst vice and malice let us bear sentience.

In each other's pain let us be elixir,
not a mouthful of lessons and judgment.
Rather than add to each other's struggle,
In each other's hardship let us share burden.

Let us breathe in each other's joy,
Breath shared is bliss acquired.
Let us bask in each other's rights,
Freedom is foul if it isn't shared.

Firefly Sonnet, 1750

Firefly, oh firefly,
why do you gleam so!
Who do you try to impress,
who is the object of your glow!

Oh, ye of little sight,
said the gentle little beacon!
Creatures with light eternal,
don't shine to stir public opinion.

I gleam, 'cause that's my life,
I know no other way of existence.
Puny apes gotta find an agenda,
for most are anemic of effulgence.

And you have the gall to call us bugs,
while your mind is stuck in gutter!
My fire bears proof of existence,
you carry yours as cheap souvenir.

Note: as a biologist I must mention, this is a purely poetic piece, not to be analyzed with science, for evolutionarily speaking, glowworms use their glow to warn away predators, and attract mate.

27. Gods and Goblins

Ghost Sonnet, 1751
(Parapsychology 101)

Do you believe in ghosts, someone asked.
Plenty mysteries to unfold, I replied.
Most cases, commoner curiosity gives in,
supernatural explanation is convenient.

Thus mysteries become paranormal,
despite being born of a natural world.
Question is not, is there an explanation,
but how far are you willing to unravel!

In short, there is no supernatural,
only natural yet to be understood.
If human mind perseveres long enough,
every mystery soon reveals its truth.

Bluntly put, there is no ghastlier
ghost than a wicked personality.
We are the gods, we are the goblins,
of our own elaborate story.

Sonnet 1752

You can be poetic,
and still have reason.
Simply foster the capacity,
to not submit to superstition.

I often transcend reason
into the realm of metaphor,
science isn't always mandatory
in the course of illumination.

Science has its time and place,
a fact no human can ignore.
But there is more to life's light,
than achieved by scientific oar.

Average scientist explores facts,
Great scientist explores life.
Plain goodness often defies logic,
Life comes before scientific pride.

28. What is Truth

What is Truth
(The Sonnet, 1753)

There is not one but two truths,
truth of facts and truth of good.
Truth of facts is worth the honor,
when it serves the truth of good.

Truth of facts thrives on logic,
an effective antidote to prejudice.
Where it sucks the sweetness of life,
truth of facts is carrier of malice.

Truth of facts is carrier of logic,
Truth of good is carrier of life.
Often times they cohabit the mind,
sometimes facts only undermine life.

Pride of truth is the good it does,
without which all facts are futile.
Truth of good is truth absolute,
absence of heart makes logic vile.

Status Quo
(The Sonnet, 1754)

Beyond the two civilized truths
of facts and good, there are plenty
primitive truths that plague society.
Though dominant in the modern world,
these truths do not reflect civility.

Truth of greed that ran the empire,
truth of prosperity that runs the US.
Just because it is the reality,
doesn't make it worth the respect.

Every society suffers such realities,
which they spinelessly accept as truth.
Just 'cause it's status quo doesn't make it
right, even if backed by a million poofs.

Truth is a dynamic force, not stagnant -
No truth is impervious to scrutiny.
In a world of apes, human is the outlaw -
Be the outlaw defying laws of monkeys!

29. Manavad Gita (Song of Human)

Triumphs & Superstitions
(The Sonnet, 1755)

There is no perfect culture,
no culture is immune to fallacy.
Every culture, ancient or new,
has its triumphs as well as
superstitions and conspiracies.

Amateur America landed us on the moon,
it also bears moon landing conspiracy.
Ancient India gave us yoga and ayurveda,
it also suffers from chakrik stupidity.

Arabia and India bore the earliest minds
of astronomy, algebra and philosophy,
yet neither is impervious to fundamentalism,
quite like the adolescent colonial society.

Mark of a great culture is its inclusive spirit,
take away inclusion, and culture becomes gutter.
When intolerance reigns as law, centuries old and
millennia old civilizations suffer equally together.

Manavad Gita, Sonnet
(Song of Human, 1756)

Cosmos is my koran,
Brahmand is my bible.
No writ is whole enough,
to contain mind indivisible.

All say their scripture is god-given*,
it takes holiness to find humans holy.
To surpass the superstition of *bhagavad,
is the beginning of civilized sanctity.

My holiness is in my hands,
no fantasy is my authority.
I'm not against faith of fiction,
but it's time for human based divinity.

If you need myths to sustain your holiness,
it's a lot of things, but it ain't holy.
Holiness of humans cares for the humans,
this is my song offering to humanity.

30. Untainted

Colossus
(The Sonnet, 1757)

Defying the decree of logic if need be,
I shall build mosques for the muslims.
No matter my rational stand on faith,
I shall build churches for the christians.

I have no faith of my own, but I stand
ready to die defending your right to faith.
I stand incorruptible as shield universal,
against persecution and intolerance.

I don't need to slaughter anyone,
in my propagation of light and life.
Puny apes with their sticks and stones,
bear no threat to my himalayan light.

My culture is compassion, my truth is love.
Transcending chains love stands beacon colossus.

Untainted
(The Sonnet, 1758)

Love me or hate me,
you cannot get rid of me.
Institutions come and go,
my vessel is infinity.

I gave my teens to the world,
I gave my twenties to the world,
I give my thirties to the world,
mine is not to count, but to be martyred.

Don't know how longer can I persevere,
I grow rather weary by the minute.
Monsoon of ideas never seem to cease,
but every vessel has its mortal limit.

Naskar will live on,
long after Abi is gone.
Hence, I burn untainted,
brief though I burn.

31. World Brother

World Brother
(The Sonnet, 1759)

My name is Abi in english,
in turkish it means big brother.
Indeed that's my role in the world,
by default, I am the world brother.

If a woman ever turns my head,
I might take an exception.
But by default all women are my sisters,
I am the universal safe haven.

If a man doesn't make you
feel safe, it's not a man.
If a woman doesn't make you
feel warm, it's not a woman.

In a gender fluid world these roles
could easily switch or overlap even,
but one thing is eternally certain,
presence of human is divine haven.

Naskar not Nascar
(The Sonnet, 1760)

Naskar is an alter ego,
Naskar is a calling,
a madness bigger than sanity,
not chained to one being.

Even Abi is no match for Naskar,
Abi will perish, not Naskar.
Naskar is a chemical catastrophe,
priming humans as kind thunder.

Naskar is factory of humanitarians,
imbued with wonders against malice.
Muscle up your heart, heart up your brain,
uncontaminated by leanings of prejudice.

Nascar is a race, Naskar is a journey,
voyage of sapiens ushering in humanity.
Surpassing constraints of archaic bigotry,
Naskar is Manifest Humanity.

32. Reformer Never Rich

Sonnet 1761

No recognition, no matter.
No industry, no matter.
No benefactor, no matter.
No accolades, no matter.

All I have is my mission,
only thing that keeps me going.
Got no riches, found no gratitude,
yet for some reason I keep giving.

I never got to enjoy my youth,
I got bit by the humanitarian bug.
When I did find romance later on,
before long, even she got fed up.

They call it activism,
I call it (reformer) life.
If all were selfish,
there would be no light.

Reformer Never Rich
(The Sonnet, 1762)

We are social reformers,
we'll never be rich.
Affluence is foreign to us,
best we could do is pay the bills.

We'll never be affluent,
in terms of money and materials.
Our only asset is the change we bring,
which can't be bought by mines of emeralds.

Architects of society aren't seduced by gold,
we are already high on the fumes of uplift.
One gentle smile of graceful gratitude
is enough to charge our exhausted batteries.

Yet gratitude is rare as english sunshine,
still the reformer mustn't be disheartened.
Any circus ape can do tricks for applause,
takes a human to stand smiling in damnation.

33. Prosperity

Atonement
(The Sonnet, 1763)

Prosperity of US and Europe do not count,
any moron can be prosperous exploiting others.
Build your empire by your own honest labor,
then you can command civil honor from humans.

I've built my legacy through sweat and tears,
that too without inheritance or exploitation.
The beacon I leave behind is a labor of love,
not a basket offspring of proud deception.

I got no patience left to illuminate further,
If you still do not find imperialism inhuman.
Even landing a man on the moon loses its glory,
when you consider America's baffling violations.

Achievement comes later, atonement comes first.
Takes a human to know this, not a Company custard.